STEALTH HEAl SLOW COOKER MEAL PREP COOKBOOK

Effortless Meal Prep for Maximum Nutrition and Flavor

Amelia Harper

Copyright © 2025 Amelia Harper

All rights reserved.

No part of this book may be copied, reproduced, stored in a retrieval system, or transmitted in any form or by any means—electronic, mechanical, photocopying, recording, or otherwise—without prior written permission from the publisher, except for brief quotations in reviews or articles.

This book is intended for personal use only. Every effort has been made to ensure the accuracy of the information provided, but the author and publisher assume no responsibility for any errors, omissions, or adverse effects resulting from the use of the recipes or techniques described. Readers are encouraged to consult a professional if they have any dietary or health concerns.

Table of Contents

INTRODUCTION 7
- Why Slow Cooker Meal Prep? 7
- How to Use This Cookbook 9
- Essential Tools & Ingredients for Meal Prep 11
- Tips for Maximizing Nutrition and Flavor 15

BREAKFAST 17
- Slow Cooker Apple Cinnamon Oatmeal 17
- Protein-Packed Egg Casserole 18
- Blueberry Almond Quinoa Porridge 20
- Healthy Banana Bread Muffins 21
- Sweet Potato and Kale Breakfast Hash 23
- Overnight Chia Pudding 24
- Slow Cooker Greek Yogurt 26

LUNCH 28
- Hearty Lentil and Vegetable Soup 28
- Slow Cooker Chicken Caesar Wrap Filling 30
- Quinoa and Black Bean Chili 31
- Thai Peanut Chicken Bowls 33
- Mediterranean Stuffed Peppers 35
- Butternut Squash and Carrot Soup 37
- Slow Cooker Pulled BBQ Jackfruit 39

DINNER 41
- Garlic Herb Chicken with Roasted Veggies 41

- Beef and Broccoli Stir-Fry 43
- Lemon Herb Salmon with Quinoa 45
- Creamy Tuscan White Bean Stew 47
- Slow Cooker Turkey Meatballs 49
- Spicy Chickpea and Spinach Curry 51
- Honey Garlic Shrimp with Brown Rice 53

DESSERTS 55

- Slow Cooker Baked Apples 55
- Chocolate Avocado Brownies 56
- Healthy Carrot Cake 58
- Stevia-Sweetened Rice Pudding 60
- Apple Cinnamon Bread Pudding 61
- Pumpkin Spice Protein Cake 63
- Slow Cooker Choco-Nut Fudge 65

SPECIAL DIET & PREFERENCES (GLUTEN-FREE, VEGAN, LOW-CARB, KETO, ETC.) 67

- Keto Cheesy Cauliflower Casserole 67
- Vegan Lentil & Mushroom Stew 69
- Paleo Lemon Garlic Chicken 71
- Low-Carb Buffalo Chicken Dip 73
- Dairy-Free Coconut Curry Chickpeas 75
- Whole30 Turkey and Sweet Potato Stew 77
- High-Protein Vegan Chili 79

SNACKS 81

- Savory Roasted Chickpeas 81

- Slow Cooker Spiced Nuts 82
- Homemade Granola Clusters 84
- Low-Sugar Applesauce 85
- Dark Chocolate Energy Bites 87
- Protein-Packed Hummus 89
- Chewy Peanut Butter Protein Bars 90

STEALTH HEALTH TIPS AND TRICKS 92

MEAL PREP PLANS 94

3-Day Meal Plan for Beginners 94

5-Day Meal Plan 95

7-Day Meal Plan 96

14-Day Meal Plan 97

CONCLUSION 99

INTRODUCTION

➢ Why Slow Cooker Meal Prep?

Meal prepping with a slow cooker is one of the easiest and most effective ways to save time, eat healthier, and reduce stress in the kitchen. Whether you have a busy schedule, want to eat more nutritious meals, or simply love the idea of home-cooked food without spending hours in the kitchen, a slow cooker can make meal preparation effortless.

1. Saves Time and Effort

One of the biggest advantages of slow cooker meal prep is that it requires very little hands-on time. You can add your ingredients to the slow cooker, set the timer, and let it do the work for you. Unlike stovetop or oven cooking, there is no need to stir constantly or check the food frequently. This allows you to focus on other tasks, whether it's work, family, or relaxation.

2. Makes Healthy Eating Easier

A slow cooker helps you prepare nutritious meals using whole, natural ingredients. Instead of relying on processed or fast food, you can make homemade meals packed with protein, fiber, vitamins, and minerals. By planning your meals in advance, you can also control portion sizes and avoid unhealthy last-minute food choices.

3. Saves Money

Eating out or ordering takeout can be expensive. Slow cooker meal prep allows you to buy ingredients in bulk, use budget-friendly cuts of meat, and reduce food waste. Since slow cooking makes tough meats tender and enhances flavors, you can create delicious meals without spending a lot of money.

4. Reduces Kitchen Stress

Cooking multiple meals during the week can feel overwhelming. With slow cooker meal prep, you can cook large portions at once and store leftovers for later. This means fewer dishes to wash, less time spent deciding what to cook, and more time to enjoy your meals.

5. Keeps Meals Fresh and Ready to Eat

Meal prepping with a slow cooker means you always have healthy meals available. You can refrigerate portions for the week or freeze them for later. This is perfect for busy days when you don't have time to cook but still want a homemade meal.

6. Enhances Flavor and Texture

Slow cooking allows ingredients to cook gently over several hours, which helps develop rich, deep flavors. It also makes meat tender, beans creamy, and vegetables flavorful. This means you can enjoy delicious meals without needing extra fats, salt, or artificial seasonings.

7. Works for Any Diet or Lifestyle

Whether you follow a low-carb, vegan, gluten-free, or high-protein diet, a slow cooker can help you prepare meals that fit your needs. You can customize recipes, swap ingredients, and adjust flavors to match your preferences.

➢ How to Use This Cookbook

This cookbook is designed to help you make healthy, delicious meals using a slow cooker. The recipes are simple, nutritious, and perfect for meal prepping. Whether you are cooking for yourself, your family, or planning meals for the week, this book will guide you step by step.

What You Will Find in This Cookbook

- **Easy-to-Follow Recipes** – Each recipe includes clear instructions, a list of ingredients, and cooking times.
- **Meal Prep Tips** – Many recipes have suggestions for storing and reheating meals. This helps you save time during busy days.
- **Nutritional Information** – Each recipe includes details on calories, protein, fat, and carbs to help you make informed food choices.
- **Variety of Categories** – The book includes recipes for breakfast, lunch, dinner, desserts, snacks, and special dietary needs.

How to Get the Best Results

1. **Read the Recipe First**
   Before you start cooking, read through the recipe. This helps you understand the steps and make sure you have all the ingredients.

2. **Prepare Your Ingredients**
   Chop vegetables, measure spices, and get everything ready before you begin. This makes cooking faster and easier.

3. **Use the Right Slow Cooker Size**
   If a recipe is for a large slow cooker (6 quarts or more) and you have a smaller one, adjust the ingredient amounts to fit your cooker.

4. **Follow the Cooking Times**
   Some recipes cook best on low heat for a longer time, while others need high heat for a shorter period. Follow the instructions for the best taste and texture.

5. **Store Leftovers Properly**

   Let the food cool before storing it in airtight containers. Keep meals in the fridge for up to 4 days or freeze them for longer storage.

6. **Reheat with Care**

   When reheating, use a microwave, oven, or stovetop. If reheating from frozen, let the meal thaw in the fridge overnight for even heating.

7. **Customize to Your Taste**

   Feel free to adjust spices, add more vegetables, or swap ingredients to fit your diet and preferences.

Making Meal Prep Easy

If you want to prepare meals in advance, choose recipes that store well. Cook in batches and divide meals into portions. This way, you will always have healthy food ready to eat, saving time and reducing stress.

By following these simple steps, you will get the most out of your slow cooker and enjoy delicious, healthy meals every day.

➤ Essential Tools & Ingredients for Meal Prep

Meal prep with a slow cooker is easy and convenient, but having the right tools and ingredients will make the process even smoother. Here are the essentials you need to get started.

Must-Have Tools for Meal Prep

1. Slow Cooker (Crockpot)

A good slow cooker is the most important tool for meal prep. Choose a size that fits your needs:

- **Small (2–4 quarts)** – Best for cooking meals for 1–2 people or side dishes.
- **Medium (5–6 quarts)** – Great for family meals and batch cooking.
- **Large (7+ quarts)** – Perfect for big meals, meal prepping for the week, or cooking for a crowd.

Some slow cookers have timers and keep-warm settings, which help prevent overcooking.

2. Measuring Cups and Spoons

Accurate measurements ensure your meals turn out perfect. Use measuring cups for liquids and dry ingredients, and measuring spoons for smaller amounts of spices and seasonings.

3. Sharp Knife and Cutting Board

A sharp knife makes it easier to chop vegetables, slice meat, and prepare ingredients quickly. A sturdy cutting board helps keep your workspace clean and safe.

4. Food Storage Containers

Proper storage is key to successful meal prep. Use:

- **Glass containers** for reheating meals safely.
- **Airtight plastic containers** for dry ingredients and snacks.
- **Mason jars** for soups, sauces, or overnight oats.
- **Freezer-safe bags** for storing pre-chopped ingredients or cooked meals.

5. Ladles and Tongs

Ladles help serve soups and stews easily, while tongs make it simple to grab cooked meat, vegetables, or pasta.

6. Slow Cooker Liners (Optional)

Slow cooker liners make cleaning up easier. They prevent food from sticking to the pot, saving time and effort.

7. A Good Can Opener

Many slow cooker recipes use canned ingredients like beans, tomatoes, or coconut milk. A sturdy can opener will save you frustration.

8. Labels and Markers

Labeling your prepped meals helps you keep track of dates and ingredients. Write the name of the meal and the date you prepared it to avoid wasting food.

Essential Ingredients for Meal Prep

Keeping the right ingredients in your kitchen will make meal prep fast and stress-free. Here are the basics to always have on hand:

1. Proteins (Main Ingredients for Meals)

Protein is essential for energy and muscle health. Great options for slow cooker meal prep include:

- **Chicken** (breast, thighs, or whole chicken)
- **Beef** (lean cuts, ground beef, or stew meat)
- **Pork** (tenderloin, ribs, or pulled pork)
- **Fish and Seafood** (salmon, shrimp, or white fish)
- **Plant-Based Proteins** (tofu, tempeh, lentils, and beans)

2. Vegetables (Fresh and Frozen)

Vegetables add flavor, color, and nutrition to your meals. Good choices include:

- **Root vegetables** (carrots, potatoes, sweet potatoes)
- **Leafy greens** (spinach, kale, Swiss chard)
- **Bell peppers, onions, and garlic** (great for adding taste)
- **Frozen vegetables** (peas, corn, broccoli—great for quick prep)

3. Whole Grains and Legumes

Grains and legumes help make meals filling and balanced. Keep these in your pantry:

- Brown rice, quinoa, barley
- Oats (for breakfast meal prep)
- Lentils, black beans, chickpeas

4. Healthy Fats

Healthy fats improve flavor and help with nutrient absorption. Good options include:

- **Olive oil, avocado oil, or coconut oil** (for cooking and dressings)
- **Nuts and seeds** (almonds, walnuts, chia seeds)

5. Herbs and Spices

Herbs and spices make meals taste amazing without extra salt or fat. Some must-haves:

- **Basic spices**: salt, pepper, garlic powder, onion powder
- **Flavor boosters**: paprika, cumin, chili powder, curry powder
- **Herbs**: basil, oregano, thyme, rosemary

6. Canned and Jarred Goods

Canned items are great for quick meal prep. Keep these in your pantry:

- Diced tomatoes, tomato paste

- Coconut milk (for curries and soups)
- Canned beans (black beans, kidney beans, chickpeas)

7. Broth and Stocks

A good broth adds depth to soups, stews, and sauces. You can use:

- **Chicken broth, beef broth, or vegetable broth**
- **Homemade stock for a healthier option**

8. Dairy and Dairy Alternatives

Some slow cooker recipes need dairy for creaminess and flavor:

- Greek yogurt (healthy substitute for sour cream)
- Cheese (cheddar, mozzarella, parmesan)
- Milk or dairy-free options (almond, soy, or oat milk)

Final Tips for Meal Prep Success

✓ **Plan Ahead** – Choose recipes for the week and prepare ingredients in advance.

✓ **Batch Cook** – Make extra portions so you have meals ready to eat later.

✓ **Use the Freezer** – Store pre-cooked meals in the freezer for quick and healthy options.

✓ **Keep It Simple** – Start with easy recipes and gradually try new ones.

➢ Tips for Maximizing Nutrition and Flavor

Cooking with a slow cooker is an easy way to make healthy, delicious meals with minimal effort. However, to get the best results, you need to know how to keep the flavors rich and the nutrients intact. Here are some simple tips to help you make the most of your slow cooker meal prep.

1. Choose Fresh, Whole Ingredients

Fresh vegetables, lean proteins, whole grains, and healthy fats make the best meals. Avoid processed foods with added sugar, salt, and preservatives. Fresh ingredients not only taste better but also contain more nutrients.

2. Use Herbs and Spices for Natural Flavor

Instead of relying on salt and sugar, season your food with fresh herbs and spices. Garlic, ginger, cumin, turmeric, paprika, rosemary, and thyme can enhance the taste without adding extra calories. Herbs and spices also have antioxidants that support good health.

3. Layer Ingredients for Better Flavor

The way you place ingredients in the slow cooker affects the final taste. Place denser vegetables like carrots, potatoes, and onions at the bottom, where they will cook slowly in the juices. Meats and proteins should go on top to absorb the flavors.

4. Brown Meat and Sauté Vegetables First

For richer flavor, brown your meat in a pan before adding it to the slow cooker. Sautéing onions, garlic, and spices in a little oil first will also bring out their natural sweetness and depth of taste.

5. Use the Right Amount of Liquid

Slow cookers trap moisture, so you don't need as much liquid as you would in traditional cooking. Adding too much liquid can dilute flavors. Use just enough broth, sauce, or water to cover the ingredients partially.

6. Add Dairy and Fresh Herbs at the End

If your recipe includes dairy products like milk, cheese, or yogurt, add them in the last 30 minutes of cooking to prevent curdling. Fresh herbs like basil and cilantro also taste best when added just before serving.

7. Choose Whole Grains for Better Nutrition

Swap white rice and pasta for whole grains like quinoa, brown rice, and barley. These grains have more fiber, vitamins, and minerals, making your meals healthier and more filling.

8. Cook on Low for Better Nutrient Retention

Cooking on a low setting for a longer time helps preserve nutrients better than high heat. Slow cooking allows vitamins and minerals to stay in the food instead of breaking down from high temperatures.

9. Avoid Overcooking Vegetables

Some vegetables, like zucchini, spinach, and bell peppers, cook faster than others. Add them in the last hour of cooking to keep their texture and nutrients intact.

10. Store and Reheat Properly

Let food cool before storing it in airtight containers. Refrigerate meals within two hours to keep them fresh. When reheating, do so on low heat to maintain flavor and texture without overcooking.

By following these simple tips, you can create slow cooker meals that are not only healthy but also packed with flavor. Enjoy delicious, nutrient-rich dishes with every meal!

BREAKFAST

> ➢ Slow Cooker Apple Cinnamon Oatmeal

Ingredients:

- 2 cups rolled oats
- 4 cups unsweetened almond milk (or water)
- 2 apples, peeled and chopped
- 2 tablespoons honey or maple syrup
- 1 teaspoon cinnamon
- ½ teaspoon vanilla extract
- ¼ teaspoon salt
- ¼ cup chopped nuts (optional)
- 2 tablespoons raisins or dried cranberries (optional)

Cooking Instructions:

Add the oats, almond milk, apples, honey, cinnamon, vanilla, and salt to the slow cooker. Stir well. Cover and cook on low for 6–8 hours or high for 3–4 hours until the oats are soft and creamy. Stir before serving. Add nuts or dried fruit if desired.

Serving Size:

Makes 4 servings

Nutritional Information (Per Serving):

- Calories: 180
- Protein: 5g
- Carbohydrates: 35g
- Fiber: 5g

- Fat: 3g
- Sugar: 10g

Tips:

Use steel-cut oats for a chewier texture. Add a splash of milk before serving if the oatmeal is too thick. Store leftovers in the fridge for up to 5 days. Reheat with a little milk or water.

Possible Variations or Substitutes:

Use pears instead of apples. Swap honey for brown sugar. Add chia seeds for extra fiber. Replace almond milk with regular or oat milk.

➤ Protein-Packed Egg Casserole

Ingredients

- 8 large eggs
- ½ cup (120ml) milk (or dairy-free alternative)
- 1 cup (100g) shredded cheddar cheese (or mozzarella)
- 1 cup (150g) diced bell peppers
- 1 cup (150g) cooked turkey sausage (or chicken sausage)
- ½ cup (75g) chopped onions
- 1 cup (150g) baby spinach, chopped
- 1 teaspoon salt
- ½ teaspoon black pepper
- ½ teaspoon garlic powder
- ½ teaspoon paprika
- Cooking spray or a little olive oil for greasing

Cooking Instructions

Lightly grease the slow cooker with cooking spray or oil. In a large bowl, whisk the eggs, milk, salt, pepper, garlic powder, and paprika. Stir in the cheese, bell peppers, onions, sausage, and spinach. Pour the mixture into the slow cooker. Cover and cook on low for 4–5 hours or on high for 2–3 hours, until the eggs are set. Let it cool slightly before slicing. Serve warm.

Serving Size

Makes 6 servings.

Nutritional Information (Per Serving)

- Calories: 210
- Protein: 18g
- Carbohydrates: 5g
- Fat: 12g
- Fiber: 1g
- Sugar: 2g

Tips

- Use a slow cooker liner for easy cleanup.
- To check if it's done, insert a knife in the center—if it comes out clean, the casserole is ready.
- Let it cool before slicing to prevent it from falling apart.

Possible Variations or Substitutes

- Replace turkey sausage with cooked bacon, ham, or vegetarian sausage.
- Swap cheddar cheese for feta or Swiss cheese.
- Add mushrooms, tomatoes, or zucchini for extra vegetables.
- Use egg whites instead of whole eggs for a lower-fat option.

➢ Blueberry Almond Quinoa Porridge

Ingredients

- 1 cup quinoa, rinsed
- 2 cups almond milk (or any milk of choice)
- 1 cup water
- 2 tablespoons maple syrup or honey
- 1 teaspoon vanilla extract
- ½ teaspoon cinnamon
- 1 cup fresh or frozen blueberries
- ¼ cup sliced almonds
- 1 tablespoon chia seeds (optional)

Cooking Instructions

Add quinoa, almond milk, water, maple syrup, vanilla, and cinnamon to the slow cooker. Stir to combine. Cover and cook on low for 4–5 hours or until the quinoa is soft and creamy. Stir in the blueberries and almonds. Let it sit for 5 minutes before serving.

Serving Size

Makes 4 servings.

Nutritional Information (Per Serving)

- Calories: 220
- Protein: 7g
- Carbohydrates: 38g
- Fiber: 5g

- Fat: 6g
- Sugar: 10g

Tips

Use frozen blueberries if fresh ones are not available. Stir occasionally if you are home to prevent sticking. If the porridge gets too thick, add a little more milk before serving.

Possible Variations or Substitutes

Use coconut milk instead of almond milk for a creamier texture. Replace blueberries with strawberries, raspberries, or chopped apples. Swap almonds for walnuts or pecans. Add a spoonful of peanut butter for extra flavor.

➢ Healthy Banana Bread Muffins

Ingredients

- 3 ripe bananas, mashed
- 2 eggs
- ¼ cup honey or maple syrup
- ⅓ cup unsweetened applesauce
- 1 teaspoon vanilla extract
- 1 ½ cups whole wheat flour
- 1 teaspoon baking soda
- ½ teaspoon baking powder
- ½ teaspoon cinnamon
- ¼ teaspoon salt

- ⅓ cup chopped walnuts or dark chocolate chips (optional)

Cooking Instructions

Mash the bananas in a large bowl. Add eggs, honey, applesauce, and vanilla. Mix well. Add whole wheat flour, baking soda, baking powder, cinnamon, and salt. Stir until combined. Fold in walnuts or chocolate chips if using. Line a muffin tin with paper liners or grease lightly. Fill each cup about three-quarters full. Cook in a slow cooker on high for 2 hours or until a toothpick inserted in the center comes out clean. Let cool before serving.

Serving Size

Makes 12 muffins.

Nutritional Information (Per Muffin)

- Calories: 120
- Protein: 3g
- Carbohydrates: 22g
- Fiber: 3g
- Sugar: 8g
- Fat: 3g

Tips

Use very ripe bananas for extra sweetness. Do not overmix the batter to keep the muffins soft. Store in an airtight container for up to 3 days or freeze for longer storage.

Possible Variations or Substitutes

Replace whole wheat flour with oat flour for a gluten-free option. Swap honey with mashed dates for natural sweetness. Add raisins, shredded coconut, or chia seeds for extra texture.

➢ Sweet Potato and Kale Breakfast Hash

Ingredients:

- 2 medium sweet potatoes, peeled and diced
- 1 small onion, chopped
- 1 red bell pepper, chopped
- 2 cups kale, chopped
- 2 cloves garlic, minced
- 4 eggs (optional)
- 1 teaspoon olive oil
- 1 teaspoon smoked paprika
- ½ teaspoon salt
- ½ teaspoon black pepper
- ½ teaspoon cumin
- ½ teaspoon chili flakes (optional)

Cooking Instructions:

Add sweet potatoes, onion, bell pepper, and garlic to the slow cooker. Drizzle with olive oil and mix well. Add smoked paprika, salt, black pepper, cumin, and chili flakes. Stir everything together. Cover and cook on low for 4 hours or high for 2 hours until the sweet potatoes are soft. Stir in the kale and let it cook for 10 more minutes until wilted. If adding eggs, crack them on top, cover, and cook for 15 minutes or until set. Serve warm.

Serving Size:

Makes 4 servings

Nutritional Information (Per Serving):

- Calories: 220

- Protein: 7g
- Carbohydrates: 35g
- Fiber: 6g
- Fat: 6g

Tips:

Use baby kale for a milder taste. If you like crispy edges, transfer to a pan and sauté for a few minutes before serving.

Possible Variations or Substitutes:

Use spinach instead of kale. Swap sweet potatoes for regular potatoes. Add cooked sausage or black beans for extra protein. Replace eggs with tofu for a vegan option.

➢ Overnight Chia Pudding

Ingredients:

- ½ cup chia seeds
- 2 cups unsweetened almond milk (or any milk of choice)
- 2 tbsp honey or maple syrup
- 1 tsp vanilla extract
- ½ tsp cinnamon (optional)
- Fresh fruits for topping (berries, banana, mango, etc.)
- Nuts or seeds for garnish (almonds, walnuts, sunflower seeds)

Cooking Instructions:

In a mixing bowl, combine chia seeds, almond milk, honey, vanilla extract, and cinnamon. Stir well to prevent clumping. Let the mixture sit for 5 minutes, then stir again to ensure the seeds are evenly distributed. Cover and refrigerate for at least 4 hours or overnight until thickened. Stir before serving and top with fresh fruits, nuts, or seeds.

Serving Size:

Makes 2 servings

Nutritional Information (Per Serving):

- Calories: 200
- Protein: 6g
- Carbohydrates: 25g
- Fiber: 10g
- Fat: 8g

Tips:

- Stir the mixture twice within the first 10 minutes to prevent lumps.
- Adjust the sweetness by adding more or less honey or maple syrup.
- Store in the refrigerator for up to 4 days in an airtight container.

Possible Variations or Substitutes:

- Use coconut milk or oat milk instead of almond milk.
- Replace honey with agave syrup for a vegan option.
- Add cocoa powder for a chocolate version.
- Mix in yogurt for a creamier texture.

➤ Slow Cooker Greek Yogurt

Ingredients

- 4 cups (1 liter) whole milk
- 2 tablespoons plain yogurt with live active cultures (as a starter)
- 1 tablespoon honey or maple syrup (optional, for slight sweetness)

Cooking Instructions

Pour the milk into the slow cooker and heat on low for about 2 hours until it reaches 180°F (82°C). Turn off the slow cooker and let the milk cool to about 110°F (43°C), which takes around 1 to 2 hours. In a small bowl, mix the plain yogurt with a few tablespoons of the warm milk, then stir it back into the slow cooker. Cover with a lid and wrap the slow cooker in a towel to keep it warm. Let it sit for 8 to 12 hours or overnight. The longer it sits, the tangier it will be. Once set, refrigerate for at least 4 hours before eating. For thicker Greek yogurt, strain it through a cheesecloth for a few hours.

Serving Size

Makes about 4 servings (1 cup per serving).

Nutritional Information (Per Serving)

- Calories: 150
- Protein: 8g
- Carbohydrates: 12g
- Fat: 8g
- Calcium: 25% of daily value

Tips

Use whole milk for a creamier texture. If you want a thicker Greek yogurt, strain it longer. If the yogurt is too tangy, stir in a little honey or fruit before serving. Always use a yogurt starter with live cultures for the best results.

Possible Variations or Substitutes

Use low-fat or skim milk for a lighter version. Try coconut milk or almond milk for a dairy-free option, but add a thickener like agar agar. Mix in vanilla, cinnamon, or fruit for different flavors.

LUNCH

➢ Hearty Lentil and Vegetable Soup

Ingredients

- 1 ½ cups dried lentils (green or brown), rinsed
- 1 medium onion, chopped
- 3 carrots, diced
- 2 celery stalks, chopped
- 3 garlic cloves, minced
- 1 can (14 oz/400g) diced tomatoes
- 4 cups (1 liter) vegetable broth
- 2 cups (500ml) water
- 1 teaspoon dried thyme
- 1 teaspoon ground cumin
- ½ teaspoon smoked paprika
- 1 bay leaf
- 1 teaspoon salt (adjust to taste)
- ½ teaspoon black pepper
- 2 cups chopped spinach or kale (optional)
- 1 tablespoon lemon juice (optional)

Cooking Instructions

Add all ingredients except spinach and lemon juice to the slow cooker. Stir well. Cover and cook on low for 7–8 hours or on high for 3–4 hours, until lentils and vegetables are tender. Remove the bay leaf. Stir in the spinach and lemon juice, if using. Let sit for 5 minutes before serving.

Serving Size

Makes 4–6 servings.

Nutritional Information (Per Serving)

- Calories: ~220
- Protein: ~12g
- Carbohydrates: ~38g
- Fiber: ~14g
- Fat: ~2g

Tips

For extra flavor, sauté the onion, garlic, and spices in a little oil before adding them to the slow cooker. If the soup is too thick, add more broth or water. Store leftovers in an airtight container in the fridge for up to 4 days or freeze for up to 3 months.

Possible Variations or Substitutes

Use red lentils for a softer texture. Swap kale for spinach or leave it out. Add diced potatoes or sweet potatoes for extra heartiness. Use chicken broth instead of vegetable broth for a non-vegan version.

➤ Slow Cooker Chicken Caesar Wrap Filling

Ingredients

- 2 boneless, skinless chicken breasts (about 500g)
- 1 cup (240ml) low-fat Caesar dressing
- ½ cup (50g) grated Parmesan cheese
- 1 teaspoon garlic powder
- 1 teaspoon onion powder
- ½ teaspoon black pepper
- ½ teaspoon salt (optional)
- 1 tablespoon lemon juice
- 2 tablespoons water or chicken broth

Cooking Instructions

Place the chicken breasts in the slow cooker. Pour the Caesar dressing over the chicken. Add Parmesan cheese, garlic powder, onion powder, black pepper, salt, lemon juice, and water. Cover and cook on low for 4 hours or on high for 2 hours. Shred the chicken with two forks and mix well with the sauce. Let it sit for 10 minutes before serving.

Serving Size

Makes 4 servings.

Nutritional Information (Per Serving)

- Calories: 220
- Protein: 28g
- Fat: 10g
- Carbohydrates: 3g
- Fiber: 0g

- Sodium: 450mg

Tips

- Use a hand mixer to shred the chicken quickly.
- Let the chicken rest in the sauce after shredding to absorb more flavor.
- If the sauce is too thick, add a little more water or chicken broth.

Possible Variations or Substitutes

- Replace Caesar dressing with Greek yogurt for a lighter version.
- Use rotisserie chicken instead of slow-cooked chicken for a faster meal.
- Add chopped lettuce or tomatoes for extra freshness.
- Serve on whole wheat tortillas, lettuce wraps, or over a salad instead of regular wraps.

➤ Quinoa and Black Bean Chili

Ingredients:

- 1 cup quinoa, rinsed
- 2 cans (15 oz each) black beans, drained and rinsed
- 1 can (15 oz) diced tomatoes
- 1 can (15 oz) tomato sauce
- 1 cup vegetable broth
- 1 cup corn kernels (fresh or frozen)
- 1 bell pepper, chopped
- 1 small onion, chopped
- 3 cloves garlic, minced

- 1 tablespoon olive oil
- 1 teaspoon ground cumin
- 1 teaspoon smoked paprika
- 1 teaspoon chili powder
- ½ teaspoon salt
- ½ teaspoon black pepper

Cooking Instructions:

Heat olive oil in a pan over medium heat. Add onion, garlic, and bell pepper. Sauté for 3 minutes until soft. Transfer to the slow cooker. Add quinoa, black beans, diced tomatoes, tomato sauce, vegetable broth, corn, cumin, paprika, chili powder, salt, and pepper. Stir well. Cover and cook on low for 6 hours or high for 3 hours. Stir before serving.

Serving Size:

Makes 4 servings

Nutritional Information (Per Serving):

- Calories: 320
- Protein: 12g
- Carbohydrates: 52g
- Fiber: 12g
- Fat: 6g

Tips:

- Rinse quinoa before cooking to remove bitterness.
- Adjust spice level by adding more or less chili powder.
- Let the chili sit for 10 minutes after cooking to thicken.

Possible Variations or Substitutes:

- Replace black beans with kidney beans or chickpeas.
- Use sweet potatoes instead of quinoa for a different texture.
- Add cooked shredded chicken for extra protein.
- Use beef or chicken broth instead of vegetable broth if preferred.

➤ Thai Peanut Chicken Bowls

Ingredients:

- 2 boneless, skinless chicken breasts (cut into bite-sized pieces)
- 1 cup (240 ml) coconut milk
- ½ cup (120 ml) natural peanut butter
- 2 tbsp soy sauce
- 1 tbsp honey or maple syrup
- 1 tbsp rice vinegar
- 1 tbsp lime juice
- 2 cloves garlic (minced)
- 1 tsp grated ginger
- ½ tsp red pepper flakes (optional, for spice)
- 1 red bell pepper (sliced)
- 1 cup (150 g) shredded carrots
- 2 cups (380 g) cooked brown rice or quinoa
- ¼ cup (30 g) chopped peanuts (for garnish)
- 2 tbsp chopped cilantro (for garnish)

Cooking Instructions:

Place the chicken, coconut milk, peanut butter, soy sauce, honey, rice vinegar, lime juice, garlic, ginger, and red pepper flakes into the slow cooker. Stir well to combine. Cover and cook on low for 4-5 hours or on high for 2-3 hours until the chicken is tender. Add the bell pepper and shredded carrots in the last 30 minutes of cooking. Serve over cooked brown rice or quinoa. Garnish with chopped peanuts and cilantro before serving.

Serving Size:

Makes 4 servings.

Nutritional Information (Per Serving):

- Calories: 420
- Protein: 32 g
- Carbohydrates: 35 g
- Fat: 18 g
- Fiber: 5 g
- Sugar: 8 g

Tips:

- Use chicken thighs instead of chicken breasts for a juicier texture.
- If you prefer a thinner sauce, add ¼ cup (60 ml) of water or broth.
- Adjust the spice level by adding more or less red pepper flakes.

Possible Variations or Substitutes:

- Swap peanut butter for almond or cashew butter if needed.
- Use tofu instead of chicken for a vegetarian version.
- Serve with cauliflower rice for a lower-carb option.

➢ Mediterranean Stuffed Peppers

Ingredients

- 4 large bell peppers (red, yellow, or green)
- 1 cup cooked quinoa or brown rice
- 1 can (15 oz) chickpeas, drained and rinsed
- 1 small onion, finely chopped
- 2 cloves garlic, minced
- 1 cup cherry tomatoes, chopped
- ½ cup crumbled feta cheese (optional)
- ¼ cup black or green olives, chopped
- 2 tablespoons olive oil
- 1 teaspoon dried oregano
- 1 teaspoon ground cumin
- ½ teaspoon salt
- ¼ teaspoon black pepper
- 1 cup vegetable broth

Cooking Instructions

Cut the tops off the bell peppers and remove the seeds. In a bowl, mix quinoa, chickpeas, onion, garlic, cherry tomatoes, feta, olives, olive oil, oregano, cumin, salt, and black pepper. Stuff the mixture into the peppers. Place them in the slow cooker and pour the vegetable broth around them. Cover and cook on low for 5–6 hours or on high for 2–3 hours until the peppers are tender. Serve warm.

Serving Size

- Makes 4 servings

Nutritional Information (Per Serving)

- Calories: 250
- Protein: 9g
- Carbohydrates: 35g
- Fiber: 7g
- Fat: 9g

Tips

- Choose firm bell peppers so they hold their shape during cooking.
- For a richer flavor, sauté the onion and garlic before mixing them with the filling.
- If you like a softer texture, cook for an additional 30 minutes.

Possible Variations or Substitutes

- Replace quinoa with couscous, bulgur, or white rice.
- Use white beans or lentils instead of chickpeas.
- Swap feta cheese for goat cheese or leave it out for a vegan option.
- Add chopped spinach or zucchini for extra vegetables.

➢ Butternut Squash and Carrot Soup

Ingredients

- 1 medium butternut squash, peeled, seeded, and chopped
- 3 large carrots, peeled and sliced
- 1 small onion, chopped
- 3 cloves garlic, minced
- 4 cups (1 liter) vegetable broth
- 1 cup (240 ml) coconut milk (optional for creaminess)
- 1 teaspoon salt
- ½ teaspoon black pepper
- ½ teaspoon ground cumin
- ½ teaspoon ground ginger
- 1 tablespoon olive oil
- 1 tablespoon lemon juice (optional for extra freshness)

Cooking Instructions

Add all ingredients except the coconut milk and lemon juice into the slow cooker. Stir to mix. Cover and cook on low for 6-7 hours or high for 3-4 hours until the vegetables are soft. Blend the soup using an immersion blender or transfer to a regular blender. Stir in the coconut milk and lemon juice. Taste and adjust seasoning if needed. Serve warm.

Serving Size

Makes 4-6 servings.

Nutritional Information (Per Serving)

- Calories: ~150
- Protein: 2g

- Carbohydrates: 25g
- Fiber: 5g
- Fat: 6g

Tips

- For extra flavor, roast the squash and carrots before adding them to the slow cooker.
- Use an immersion blender for easy blending.
- Store leftovers in an airtight container in the fridge for up to 4 days or freeze for up to 3 months.

Possible Variations or Substitutes

- Replace coconut milk with heavy cream or Greek yogurt.
- Use sweet potatoes instead of butternut squash.
- Add red pepper flakes for a spicier taste.

➢ Slow Cooker Pulled BBQ Jackfruit

Ingredients

- 2 cans (14 oz each) young green jackfruit in water or brine, drained and rinsed
- 1 small onion, finely chopped
- 3 cloves garlic, minced
- 1 cup (240 ml) BBQ sauce (your favorite)
- ½ cup (120 ml) vegetable broth or water
- 1 tbsp olive oil
- 1 tbsp apple cider vinegar
- 1 tbsp maple syrup or honey
- 1 tsp smoked paprika
- 1 tsp ground cumin
- ½ tsp black pepper
- ½ tsp salt

Cooking Instructions

Heat olive oil in a pan over medium heat. Add onion and garlic. Cook for 2 minutes until soft. Transfer to the slow cooker. Add jackfruit, BBQ sauce, broth, vinegar, maple syrup, paprika, cumin, pepper, and salt. Stir well. Cover and cook on low for 4–5 hours or on high for 2–3 hours. After cooking, use two forks to shred the jackfruit. Stir well and let it sit for 10 minutes to absorb more flavor. Serve on buns, in tacos, or over rice.

Serving Size

Makes 4 servings

Nutritional Information (Per Serving)

- Calories: 180

- Protein: 2g
- Carbohydrates: 38g
- Fat: 3g
- Fiber: 6g
- Sugar: 18g
- Sodium: 480mg

Tips

- For extra flavor, let the jackfruit marinate in the sauce for 30 minutes before cooking.
- If using jackfruit in brine, rinse well to remove the salty taste.
- For a thicker sauce, remove the lid in the last 20 minutes of cooking.

Possible Variations or Substitutes

- Use soy sauce instead of salt for a deeper flavor.
- Replace BBQ sauce with teriyaki sauce for an Asian-style dish.
- Add chili powder for extra spice.
- Use shredded chicken or mushrooms instead of jackfruit if preferred.

DINNER

➢ Garlic Herb Chicken with Roasted Veggies

Ingredients

- 4 boneless, skinless chicken breasts
- 3 cups mixed vegetables (carrots, bell peppers, zucchini, broccoli)
- 3 tablespoons olive oil
- 4 cloves garlic, minced
- 1 teaspoon dried oregano
- 1 teaspoon dried thyme
- 1 teaspoon dried rosemary
- 1 teaspoon paprika
- 1 teaspoon salt
- ½ teaspoon black pepper
- ½ teaspoon red pepper flakes (optional)
- 1 lemon, sliced

Cooking Instructions

Place the chicken breasts in the slow cooker. In a small bowl, mix olive oil, garlic, oregano, thyme, rosemary, paprika, salt, black pepper, and red pepper flakes. Rub this mixture over the chicken. Add the mixed vegetables around the chicken. Place lemon slices on top. Cover and cook on **low for 6 hours** or **high for 3 hours** until the chicken is fully cooked and tender. Serve warm.

Serving Size

- Serves **4 people**

Nutritional Information *(Per Serving)*

- Calories: **320**
- Protein: **40g**
- Carbohydrates: **12g**
- Fiber: **4g**
- Fat: **12g**

Tips

Use fresh herbs instead of dried ones for a stronger flavor. For extra crispiness, transfer the cooked chicken and veggies to a baking sheet and broil for 5 minutes. Serve with brown rice or quinoa for a complete meal.

Possible Variations or Substitutes

Use **chicken thighs** instead of breasts for juicier meat. Swap the **vegetables** based on preference, such as sweet potatoes, cauliflower, or asparagus. Replace **olive oil** with avocado oil for a different taste. Add **Parmesan cheese** on top before serving for extra flavor.

➤ Beef and Broccoli Stir-Fry

Ingredients:

- 1 lb (450g) beef sirloin or flank steak, thinly sliced
- 4 cups (300g) broccoli florets
- 1 cup (240ml) low-sodium beef broth
- ¼ cup (60ml) low-sodium soy sauce
- 2 tablespoons oyster sauce (optional)
- 1 tablespoon honey or brown sugar
- 1 tablespoon cornstarch
- 1 tablespoon water
- 1 teaspoon sesame oil
- 3 cloves garlic, minced
- 1 teaspoon grated ginger
- ½ teaspoon red pepper flakes (optional)
- 2 tablespoons sesame seeds (for garnish)
- 2 green onions, sliced (for garnish)

Cooking Instructions:

Place the beef slices in the slow cooker. Add beef broth, soy sauce, oyster sauce, honey, garlic, ginger, sesame oil, and red pepper flakes. Stir to coat the beef evenly. Cover and cook on low for 4–5 hours or until the beef is tender. Mix cornstarch with water and stir it into the slow cooker. Add broccoli and mix well. Cover and cook for another 20–30 minutes until the sauce thickens and the broccoli is tender. Serve hot, garnished with sesame seeds and green onions.

Serving Size:

Makes 4 servings.

Nutritional Information (Per Serving):

- Calories: 280
- Protein: 30g
- Carbohydrates: 18g
- Fat: 10g
- Fiber: 3g
- Sodium: 500mg

Tips:

- Slice the beef thinly to ensure it cooks evenly and stays tender.
- For extra flavor, brown the beef in a pan before adding it to the slow cooker.
- If you prefer a thicker sauce, add an extra teaspoon of cornstarch mixed with water.

Possible Variations or Substitutes:

- Replace beef with chicken or tofu for a different protein option.
- Use tamari or coconut aminos instead of soy sauce for a gluten-free version.
- Swap honey for maple syrup or omit it for a low-carb option.
- Add bell peppers or carrots for extra vegetables.

➤ Lemon Herb Salmon with Quinoa

Ingredients

- 4 salmon fillets (about 150g each)
- 1 cup quinoa, rinsed
- 2 cups vegetable or chicken broth
- 2 tablespoons olive oil
- Juice of 1 lemon
- 1 teaspoon lemon zest
- 3 garlic cloves, minced
- 1 teaspoon dried oregano
- 1 teaspoon dried thyme
- ½ teaspoon salt
- ½ teaspoon black pepper
- 1 cup cherry tomatoes, halved
- 1 cup baby spinach
- ½ teaspoon chili flakes (optional)

Cooking Instructions

Add quinoa and broth to the slow cooker. Stir and spread evenly. Place salmon fillets on top. Drizzle olive oil and lemon juice over the salmon. Sprinkle with lemon zest, garlic, oregano, thyme, salt, and black pepper. Cover and cook on low for 2 hours or until the salmon flakes easily with a fork. Add cherry tomatoes and spinach in the last 15 minutes. Serve warm.

Serving Size

4 servings

Nutritional Information (Per Serving)

- Calories: 380
- Protein: 35g
- Carbohydrates: 30g
- Fat: 15g
- Fiber: 4g
- Sodium: 400mg

Tips

Use fresh salmon for better flavor. If the salmon is frozen, thaw it before cooking. Add a little more lemon juice before serving for extra freshness.

Possible Variations or Substitutes

Use brown rice instead of quinoa, but increase the cooking time. Swap spinach for kale or arugula. Replace salmon with trout or cod.

Creamy Tuscan White Bean Stew

Ingredients

- 2 cans (15 oz each) white beans, drained and rinsed
- 1 small onion, finely chopped
- 3 cloves garlic, minced
- 1 medium carrot, diced
- 2 cups vegetable broth
- 1 cup unsweetened coconut milk or heavy cream
- 2 cups fresh spinach, chopped
- 1 can (14 oz) diced tomatoes, drained
- 1 teaspoon dried oregano
- 1 teaspoon dried basil
- ½ teaspoon red pepper flakes (optional)
- 2 tablespoons olive oil
- Salt and black pepper to taste

Cooking Instructions

Heat olive oil in the slow cooker on the sauté setting or in a pan over medium heat. Add onion, garlic, and carrot. Cook for 3-4 minutes until softened. Transfer to the slow cooker. Add white beans, vegetable broth, diced tomatoes, oregano, basil, red pepper flakes, salt, and black pepper. Stir well. Cover and cook on low for 6-7 hours or high for 3-4 hours. Stir in coconut milk and spinach 15 minutes before serving. Adjust seasoning if needed. Serve hot.

Serving Size

Serves 4

Nutritional Information (Per Serving)

- Calories: 280
- Protein: 10g
- Carbohydrates: 35g
- Fat: 12g
- Fiber: 8g
- Sugar: 6g

Tips

- For extra creaminess, blend half of the beans before adding them.
- Add a squeeze of lemon juice before serving for a fresh flavor.
- Serve with whole-grain bread for a complete meal.

Possible Variations or Substitutes

- Replace spinach with kale or Swiss chard.
- Use cannellini, great northern, or navy beans.
- Swap coconut milk with heavy cream or cashew cream.
- Add cooked chicken or sausage for extra protein.

➢ Slow Cooker Turkey Meatballs

Ingredients

- 1 lb (450g) ground turkey
- ½ cup breadcrumbs (or oat flour for gluten-free)
- 1 egg
- ¼ cup grated Parmesan cheese (optional)
- 2 cloves garlic, minced
- ½ teaspoon salt
- ½ teaspoon black pepper
- 1 teaspoon dried oregano
- 1 teaspoon dried basil
- ½ teaspoon paprika
- 1 tablespoon olive oil
- 1 (24 oz / 700g) jar tomato sauce
- ½ cup water

Cooking Instructions

In a bowl, mix ground turkey, breadcrumbs, egg, Parmesan (if using), garlic, salt, pepper, oregano, basil, and paprika. Roll into small meatballs. Heat olive oil in a pan over medium heat and brown the meatballs for 2 minutes on each side. Pour half of the tomato sauce into the slow cooker. Place the meatballs inside and pour the remaining sauce and water over them. Cover and cook on low for 4-5 hours or high for 2-3 hours. Serve warm.

Serving Size

- Serves 4 (about 4 meatballs per serving)

Nutritional Information (Per Serving)

- Calories: 250
- Protein: 25g
- Carbohydrates: 15g
- Fat: 10g
- Fiber: 2g
- Sugar: 5g

Tips

- Browning the meatballs first gives them better texture and flavor.
- Use lean turkey for a lighter meal or mix with ground chicken for variety.
- Add chopped spinach or shredded zucchini for extra nutrients.

Possible Variations or Substitutes

- Use ground beef or chicken instead of turkey.
- Swap breadcrumbs for almond flour to make it low-carb.
- Replace tomato sauce with a creamy sauce for a different flavor.

➢ Spicy Chickpea and Spinach Curry

Ingredients

- 2 cans (400g each) chickpeas, drained and rinsed
- 2 cups (60g) fresh spinach
- 1 can (400g) diced tomatoes
- 1 cup (240ml) coconut milk
- 1 onion, finely chopped
- 3 cloves garlic, minced
- 1-inch (2.5cm) piece of ginger, grated
- 1 tablespoon olive oil
- 1 teaspoon cumin
- 1 teaspoon turmeric
- 1 teaspoon paprika
- 1 teaspoon garam masala
- ½ teaspoon chili flakes (adjust to taste)
- ½ teaspoon salt (or to taste)
- ½ teaspoon black pepper
- ½ cup (120ml) vegetable broth or water
- Juice of ½ lemon

Cooking Instructions

Heat olive oil in the slow cooker on sauté mode or in a pan. Add onion, garlic, and ginger, then cook for 2–3 minutes until soft. Stir in cumin, turmeric, paprika, garam masala, and chili flakes. Cook for 1 minute until fragrant. Add diced tomatoes, chickpeas, coconut milk, vegetable broth, salt, and pepper. Stir well. Cover and cook on low for 6 hours or high for 3 hours. Stir in spinach and lemon juice in the last 10 minutes. Serve hot.

Serving Size

Makes 4 servings.

Nutritional Information (Per Serving)

- Calories: 280
- Protein: 10g
- Carbohydrates: 35g
- Fat: 12g
- Fiber: 9g
- Sugar: 6g
- Sodium: 450mg

Tips

- If you like a thicker curry, mash some of the chickpeas with a spoon before serving.
- Adjust the spice level by adding more or less chili flakes.
- For extra flavor, toast the spices in the pan before adding them to the slow cooker.

Possible Variations or Substitutes

- Replace spinach with kale or Swiss chard.
- Use dried chickpeas (soaked overnight) instead of canned chickpeas.
- Swap coconut milk with Greek yogurt for a lower-fat option.
- Add diced potatoes or bell peppers for more texture.

Honey Garlic Shrimp with Brown Rice

Ingredients

- 1 pound (450g) shrimp, peeled and deveined
- 1 cup (180g) brown rice
- 2 cups (480ml) water or low-sodium broth
- 3 tablespoons honey
- 3 tablespoons low-sodium soy sauce
- 2 cloves garlic, minced
- 1 teaspoon grated ginger
- 1 tablespoon olive oil
- ½ teaspoon red pepper flakes (optional)
- 1 tablespoon cornstarch mixed with 2 tablespoons water (optional, for thickening)
- 2 green onions, sliced (for garnish)
- 1 teaspoon sesame seeds (for garnish)

Cooking Instructions

Rinse the brown rice and add it to the slow cooker with water or broth. Cover and cook on low for 3 hours or until tender. In a bowl, mix honey, soy sauce, garlic, ginger, and red pepper flakes. Heat olive oil in a pan over medium heat. Add shrimp and cook for 2 minutes per side. Pour the honey garlic sauce over the shrimp and cook for 3 more minutes. If a thicker sauce is desired, stir in the cornstarch mixture and simmer until thickened. Serve the shrimp over brown rice and garnish with green onions and sesame seeds.

Serving Size

- Serves 4

Nutritional Information (Per Serving)

- Calories: 320
- Protein: 28g
- Carbohydrates: 45g
- Fat: 6g
- Fiber: 3g
- Sodium: 480mg

Tips

- Use frozen shrimp if fresh is unavailable. Thaw before cooking.
- For extra flavor, marinate the shrimp in the sauce for 15 minutes before cooking.
- Adjust sweetness by adding more or less honey.

Possible Variations or Substitutes

- Replace brown rice with quinoa or cauliflower rice for a low-carb option.
- Swap shrimp for chicken or tofu.
- Use coconut aminos instead of soy sauce for a soy-free version.

DESSERTS

➢ Slow Cooker Baked Apples

Ingredients

- 4 large apples (Honeycrisp, Fuji, or Granny Smith)
- ¼ cup rolled oats
- ¼ cup chopped walnuts or pecans
- 2 tablespoons honey or maple syrup
- 1 teaspoon cinnamon
- ½ teaspoon vanilla extract
- ¼ teaspoon nutmeg (optional)
- 2 tablespoons raisins or dried cranberries
- ½ cup water

Cooking Instructions

Core the apples, leaving the bottom intact to hold the filling. In a bowl, mix oats, nuts, honey, cinnamon, vanilla, nutmeg, and raisins. Fill each apple with the mixture and place them in the slow cooker. Pour water into the slow cooker. Cover and cook on low for 3 to 4 hours or until the apples are tender. Serve warm.

Serving Size

Makes 4 servings (1 apple per person).

Nutritional Information (Per Serving)

- Calories: 180
- Protein: 2g
- Carbohydrates: 40g

- Fiber: 5g
- Sugar: 25g
- Fat: 5g

Tips

Use firm apples to prevent them from becoming too soft. For extra flavor, drizzle with Greek yogurt or almond butter before serving. Store leftovers in the fridge for up to 3 days.

Possible Variations or Substitutes

Use pears instead of apples for a different taste. Replace honey with agave syrup for a vegan option. Swap walnuts for sunflower seeds if you need a nut-free version. Add a pinch of ginger for extra warmth.

➢ Chocolate Avocado Brownies

Ingredients

- 2 ripe avocados
- ½ cup (120ml) honey or maple syrup
- 2 eggs
- 1 teaspoon vanilla extract
- ½ cup (50g) unsweetened cocoa powder
- ½ teaspoon baking soda
- ¼ teaspoon salt
- ½ cup (60g) almond flour or whole wheat flour
- ½ cup (90g) dark chocolate chips

Cooking Instructions

Mash the avocados until smooth. Add honey, eggs, and vanilla extract. Mix well. Stir in cocoa powder, baking soda, salt, and flour. Mix until combined. Fold in chocolate chips. Grease the slow cooker and pour the batter inside. Spread evenly. Cover and cook on low for 2 to 3 hours, or until a toothpick comes out clean. Let cool before slicing.

Serving Size

Makes 9 brownies.

Nutritional Information (Per Brownie)

- Calories: 180
- Protein: 4g
- Carbohydrates: 22g
- Fat: 10g
- Fiber: 3g
- Sugar: 12g

Tips

- Use very ripe avocados for a smooth texture.
- For a richer taste, add 1 tablespoon of brewed coffee to the batter.
- To make slicing easier, let the brownies cool completely.

Possible Variations and Substitutes

- Replace honey with coconut sugar for a lower glycemic option.
- Use flax eggs (1 tablespoon flaxseed + 3 tablespoons water per egg) for a vegan version.
- Swap almond flour with oat flour if preferred.
- Add walnuts or pecans for extra crunch.

➢ Healthy Carrot Cake

Ingredients

- 2 cups (250g) whole wheat flour
- 1 ½ teaspoons baking powder
- 1 teaspoon baking soda
- 1 teaspoon cinnamon
- ½ teaspoon nutmeg
- ¼ teaspoon salt
- 2 cups (220g) grated carrots
- ½ cup (120ml) unsweetened applesauce
- ½ cup (120ml) honey or maple syrup
- ⅓ cup (80ml) olive oil or melted coconut oil
- 2 eggs
- 1 teaspoon vanilla extract
- ½ cup (120ml) milk (dairy or plant-based)
- ½ cup (60g) chopped walnuts or pecans (optional)
- ¼ cup (40g) raisins (optional)

Cooking Instructions

Grease the slow cooker with oil or use parchment paper. In a bowl, mix flour, baking powder, baking soda, cinnamon, nutmeg, and salt. In another bowl, whisk eggs, applesauce, honey, oil, vanilla, and milk. Add grated carrots and mix well. Slowly add the dry ingredients and stir until combined. Fold in nuts and raisins if using. Pour the batter into the slow cooker. Cover and cook on low for 2 ½ to 3 hours, or until a toothpick comes out clean. Turn off the slow cooker and let the cake rest for 15 minutes before removing.

Serving Size

Makes 8 servings.

Nutritional Information (Per Serving)

- Calories: 220
- Protein: 4g
- Carbohydrates: 32g
- Fiber: 4g
- Sugar: 14g
- Fat: 9g

Tips

- Use a clean towel under the slow cooker lid to absorb moisture and prevent a soggy top.
- Let the cake cool completely before slicing for a better texture.
- Store leftovers in an airtight container for up to 4 days.

Possible Variations or Substitutes

- Replace whole wheat flour with almond flour for a gluten-free option.
- Use mashed bananas instead of applesauce for a different flavor.
- Swap honey for stevia or monk fruit sweetener for a lower-sugar version.

➢ Stevia-Sweetened Rice Pudding

Ingredients

- 1 cup (200g) uncooked white rice (jasmine or arborio)
- 4 cups (1 liter) unsweetened almond milk (or regular milk)
- ¼ cup (50ml) water
- 2 tbsp granulated stevia (adjust to taste)
- 1 tsp vanilla extract
- ½ tsp ground cinnamon
- ¼ tsp salt
- ½ cup (80g) raisins (optional)

Cooking Instructions

Add rice, almond milk, and water to the slow cooker. Stir well. Cover and cook on low for 2–3 hours until the rice is soft and creamy. Stir occasionally to prevent sticking. Add stevia, vanilla extract, cinnamon, and salt. Stir well. If using raisins, mix them in. Cover and cook for another 15–20 minutes. Serve warm or chilled.

Serving Size

Makes 4 servings.

Nutritional Information (Per Serving)

- Calories: 180
- Protein: 4g
- Carbohydrates: 35g
- Fiber: 1g
- Sugar: 5g
- Fat: 3g

Tips

Use full-fat coconut milk for a richer texture. Stir frequently in the last 30 minutes to prevent the rice from sticking. If the pudding is too thick, add more milk before serving.

Possible Variations or Substitutes

Use brown rice instead of white for more fiber. Replace almond milk with oat or coconut milk. Swap raisins for chopped dates or nuts for extra texture. Add nutmeg or cardamom for a different flavor.

➢ Apple Cinnamon Bread Pudding

Ingredients:

- 6 cups (about 300g) of whole wheat or white bread, cut into cubes
- 2 large apples, peeled and chopped
- 2 cups (500ml) of milk (or almond milk for dairy-free)
- 3 large eggs
- ½ cup (100g) of brown sugar (or honey)
- 1 teaspoon of cinnamon
- 1 teaspoon of vanilla extract
- ¼ teaspoon of salt
- ¼ cup (60g) of raisins (optional)
- 2 tablespoons of melted butter (or coconut oil for dairy-free)

Cooking Instructions:

Grease the slow cooker with butter or oil. In a large bowl, whisk the milk, eggs, sugar, cinnamon, vanilla, and salt. Add the bread cubes and mix well. Stir in the chopped apples and raisins. Pour everything into the slow cooker and drizzle with melted butter. Cover and cook on low for 3–4 hours, or until the pudding is set. Serve warm.

Serving Size:

Makes 6 servings.

Nutritional Information (Per Serving):

- Calories: 250
- Protein: 7g
- Carbohydrates: 45g
- Fat: 6g
- Fiber: 4g
- Sugar: 22g

Tips:

Use stale bread for better texture. If the pudding looks too dry, add a little more milk before cooking. For extra sweetness, drizzle with honey or maple syrup before serving.

Possible Variations or Substitutes:

- Use pears instead of apples.
- Swap brown sugar for coconut sugar.
- Add chopped nuts for crunch.
- Replace raisins with dried cranberries or chocolate chips.

➢ Pumpkin Spice Protein Cake

Ingredients

- 1 cup pumpkin purée (not pumpkin pie filling)
- 2 eggs
- ½ cup unsweetened applesauce
- ¼ cup honey or maple syrup
- 1 teaspoon vanilla extract
- 1½ cups oat flour (or blended oats)
- 1 scoop vanilla or unflavored protein powder
- 1 teaspoon baking powder
- ½ teaspoon baking soda
- 1½ teaspoons cinnamon
- ½ teaspoon nutmeg
- ¼ teaspoon ginger
- ¼ teaspoon salt

Cooking Instructions

Grease the slow cooker with oil or line it with parchment paper. In a large bowl, mix the pumpkin, eggs, applesauce, honey, and vanilla until smooth. Add oat flour, protein powder, baking powder, baking soda, cinnamon, nutmeg, ginger, and salt. Stir until combined. Pour the batter into the slow cooker. Cover and cook on **low** for **2 to 3 hours** or until a toothpick inserted in the center comes out clean. Let it cool before slicing.

Serving Size

- Makes **6 to 8 slices**

Nutritional Information (Per Slice) *(approximate values)*

- Calories: **140**
- Protein: **7g**
- Carbohydrates: **22g**
- Fat: **3g**
- Fiber: **3g**
- Sugar: **8g**

Tips

- Use a towel under the slow cooker lid to catch moisture and prevent a soggy cake.
- Let the cake cool before slicing for better texture.
- Store leftovers in an airtight container in the fridge for up to **5 days**.

Possible Variations or Substitutes

- Replace honey with stevia or monk fruit for a **lower-sugar version**.
- Swap oat flour with almond flour for a **gluten-free option**.
- Add chocolate chips or chopped nuts for extra flavor.
- Use Greek yogurt instead of applesauce for **extra protein**.

➢ Slow Cooker Choco-Nut Fudge

Ingredients:

- 2 cups (340g) dark chocolate chips (at least 70% cocoa)
- 1 cup (240ml) sweetened condensed milk
- ¼ cup (60g) unsalted butter, cut into pieces
- ½ teaspoon vanilla extract
- ½ teaspoon sea salt
- ½ cup (60g) chopped walnuts (or any nuts of choice)

Cooking Instructions:

1. Add chocolate chips, sweetened condensed milk, and butter to the slow cooker.
2. Set to **low heat** and cook for **1 to 1.5 hours**, stirring every 20 minutes until melted and smooth.
3. Turn off the heat. Stir in vanilla extract, sea salt, and chopped nuts.
4. Line a baking dish with parchment paper and pour the fudge mixture into it.
5. Spread evenly and refrigerate for at least **3 hours** until firm.
6. Cut into squares and enjoy.

Serving Size:

- Makes **16 small pieces**

Nutritional Information (per piece):

- Calories: **120**
- Protein: **2g**
- Fat: **8g**
- Carbohydrates: **12g**

- Fiber: **1g**
- Sugar: **9g**

Tips:

- Stir often while melting to prevent burning.
- Use a silicone spatula for easy mixing.
- Store in an airtight container in the fridge for up to **1 week**.

Possible Variations or Substitutes:

- Use **milk chocolate** for a sweeter taste.
- Replace **walnuts** with almonds, pecans, or hazelnuts.
- Add **dried fruit** like cranberries or raisins for extra texture.
- Use **coconut condensed milk** for a dairy-free version.

SPECIAL DIET & PREFERENCES (GLUTEN-FREE, VEGAN, LOW-CARB, KETO, ETC.)

➢ Keto Cheesy Cauliflower Casserole

Ingredients

- 1 large head of cauliflower, cut into florets (about 5 cups)
- 1 cup heavy cream
- 1 ½ cups shredded cheddar cheese
- ½ cup grated Parmesan cheese
- 4 oz cream cheese, softened
- 2 cloves garlic, minced
- ½ teaspoon salt
- ½ teaspoon black pepper
- ½ teaspoon paprika
- ½ teaspoon dried oregano
- ¼ teaspoon cayenne pepper (optional)
- ½ cup cooked and crumbled bacon (optional)
- 2 tablespoons chopped fresh parsley (for garnish)

Cooking Instructions

Add the cauliflower florets to the slow cooker. In a bowl, mix heavy cream, cream cheese, garlic, salt, pepper, paprika, oregano, and cayenne pepper until smooth. Pour the mixture over the cauliflower and stir to coat evenly. Sprinkle shredded cheddar and Parmesan cheese on top. Cover and cook on **low for 3–4 hours** or until the cauliflower is tender. If adding bacon, sprinkle it over the top in the last 30 minutes. Serve hot, garnished with fresh parsley.

Serving Size

Makes **4–6 servings**

Nutritional Information (Per Serving, Approximate)

- Calories: **320**
- Protein: **12g**
- Fat: **28g**
- Carbohydrates: **6g**
- Fiber: **2g**
- Net Carbs: **4g**

Tips

- For a crispier top, transfer the casserole to an oven-safe dish and broil for **3–5 minutes** after slow cooking.
- If you prefer a smoother texture, mash the cauliflower slightly before serving.
- Use freshly shredded cheese for better melting and flavor.

Possible Variations or Substitutes

- Use **broccoli** instead of cauliflower for a different flavor.
- Replace cheddar with **Gruyère or mozzarella** for a new taste.
- Use **coconut cream** instead of heavy cream for a dairy-free version.
- Add **chopped chicken** or turkey to make it a full meal.

➢ Vegan Lentil & Mushroom Stew

Ingredients:

- 1 ½ cups (270g) dried green or brown lentils, rinsed
- 2 cups (150g) mushrooms, sliced
- 1 medium onion, chopped
- 3 cloves garlic, minced
- 2 medium carrots, chopped
- 2 celery stalks, chopped
- 1 can (400g) diced tomatoes
- 4 cups (1 liter) vegetable broth
- 1 teaspoon dried thyme
- 1 teaspoon dried oregano
- 1 teaspoon smoked paprika
- 1 tablespoon soy sauce or tamari
- 2 tablespoons olive oil
- 1 bay leaf
- Salt and black pepper to taste
- 2 cups (60g) fresh spinach (optional)

Cooking Instructions:

Heat olive oil in a pan over medium heat. Add onions, garlic, carrots, and celery. Sauté for 3–4 minutes until softened. Transfer to the slow cooker. Add mushrooms, lentils, diced tomatoes, vegetable broth, thyme, oregano, smoked paprika, soy sauce, and the bay leaf. Stir well. Cover and cook on low for 6–7 hours or on high for 3–4 hours, until the lentils are tender. Remove the bay leaf. Stir in fresh spinach (if using) and let it wilt for 5 minutes. Season with salt and black pepper to taste. Serve warm.

Serving Size:

Makes 4–6 servings.

Nutritional Information (Per Serving):

- Calories: ~230 kcal
- Protein: ~12g
- Carbohydrates: ~35g
- Fiber: ~10g
- Fat: ~6g

Tips:

- If you want a thicker stew, mash some of the lentils with a spoon before serving.
- Let the stew cool before storing it in an airtight container. It keeps well in the fridge for up to 4 days and freezes for up to 3 months.

Possible Variations or Substitutes:

- Use red lentils for a softer texture, but reduce cooking time to 4–5 hours on low.
- Replace mushrooms with zucchini or eggplant for a different taste.
- Add a splash of coconut milk for a creamy version.

Paleo Lemon Garlic Chicken

Ingredients

- 4 boneless, skinless chicken breasts
- 4 cloves garlic, minced
- 2 tablespoons olive oil
- Juice of 2 lemons
- 1 teaspoon lemon zest
- 1 teaspoon dried oregano
- 1 teaspoon paprika
- ½ teaspoon salt
- ½ teaspoon black pepper
- ½ teaspoon red pepper flakes (optional)
- ½ cup chicken broth
- 1 tablespoon fresh parsley, chopped (for garnish)

Cooking Instructions

Rub the chicken breasts with salt, pepper, paprika, and oregano. In a pan, heat olive oil and sauté garlic for 1 minute until fragrant. Add the chicken and sear for 2 minutes on each side. Transfer to the slow cooker. Pour in the lemon juice, lemon zest, chicken broth, and red pepper flakes. Cover and cook on low for 4–5 hours or until the chicken is tender. Garnish with fresh parsley before serving.

Serving Size

4 servings

Nutritional Information (Per Serving)

- Calories: 220

- Protein: 30g
- Carbohydrates: 3g
- Fat: 9g
- Fiber: 0g

Tips

Use fresh lemon juice for the best flavor. If the sauce is too thin, let it simmer uncovered for 10 minutes after cooking. Serve with roasted vegetables or cauliflower rice for a complete paleo meal.

Possible Variations or Substitutes

Replace chicken breasts with boneless thighs for juicier meat. Use lime juice instead of lemon for a different citrus flavor. Add coconut milk for a creamy version.

➢ Low-Carb Buffalo Chicken Dip

Ingredients

- 2 cups (about 300g) shredded cooked chicken
- 1 cup (240g) cream cheese, softened
- ½ cup (120ml) hot sauce (like Frank's RedHot)
- ½ cup (120g) sour cream
- 1 cup (120g) shredded cheddar cheese
- ½ cup (60g) shredded mozzarella cheese
- ½ teaspoon garlic powder
- ½ teaspoon onion powder
- ½ teaspoon smoked paprika
- ¼ teaspoon black pepper
- 2 tablespoons chopped green onions (optional)

Cooking Instructions

Add the shredded chicken, cream cheese, hot sauce, sour cream, cheddar cheese, mozzarella cheese, garlic powder, onion powder, smoked paprika, and black pepper to the slow cooker. Stir well to combine. Cover and cook on low for 2–3 hours or until the cheese is fully melted and the dip is hot. Stir again before serving. Sprinkle with green onions if desired.

Serving Size

Makes about 6 servings.

Nutritional Information (Per Serving)

- Calories: 250
- Protein: 18g
- Fat: 20g

- Carbohydrates: 3g
- Fiber: 0g
- Sugar: 1g

Tips

- Use rotisserie chicken for faster prep.
- Adjust the hot sauce amount based on your spice preference.
- Serve with celery sticks, cucumber slices, or low-carb crackers.

Possible Variations or Substitutes

- Use Greek yogurt instead of sour cream for extra protein.
- Swap cheddar for Monterey Jack or blue cheese for a different flavor.
- Use dairy-free cream cheese and cheese alternatives for a lactose-free version.

➢ Dairy-Free Coconut Curry Chickpeas

Ingredients:

- 2 cans (15 oz each) chickpeas, drained and rinsed
- 1 can (14 oz) coconut milk
- 1 cup diced tomatoes (fresh or canned)
- 1 small onion, chopped
- 3 cloves garlic, minced
- 1-inch piece ginger, grated
- 1 cup vegetable broth
- 1 tablespoon curry powder
- 1 teaspoon turmeric
- 1 teaspoon cumin
- ½ teaspoon paprika
- ½ teaspoon salt (adjust to taste)
- ¼ teaspoon black pepper
- 1 tablespoon olive oil
- 1 cup baby spinach
- Juice of ½ lemon
- Fresh cilantro for garnish (optional)

Cooking Instructions:

Heat the olive oil in a pan and sauté the onion, garlic, and ginger for 2–3 minutes until fragrant. Transfer to the slow cooker. Add chickpeas, diced tomatoes, coconut milk, vegetable broth, curry powder, turmeric, cumin, paprika, salt, and black pepper. Stir well. Cover and cook on low for 6 hours or high for 3 hours. Stir in the baby spinach and lemon juice in the last 10 minutes. Serve hot, garnished with fresh cilantro if desired.

Serving Size:

Makes 4 servings

Nutritional Information (Per Serving):

- Calories: 320
- Protein: 10g
- Carbohydrates: 38g
- Fiber: 10g
- Fat: 14g
- Saturated Fat: 8g
- Sodium: 450mg

Tips:

- For a thicker curry, mash some of the chickpeas before serving.
- Adjust spices to taste for a milder or spicier dish.
- Serve with brown rice, quinoa, or whole-wheat naan for a complete meal.

Possible Variations or Substitutes:

- Replace chickpeas with lentils or white beans.
- Swap baby spinach for kale or Swiss chard.
- Use coconut cream instead of coconut milk for a richer texture.
- Add diced bell peppers or carrots for extra vegetables.

Whole30 Turkey and Sweet Potato Stew

Ingredients

- 1 lb (450g) ground turkey
- 2 medium sweet potatoes, peeled and diced
- 1 onion, chopped
- 3 cloves garlic, minced
- 2 carrots, sliced
- 2 celery stalks, chopped
- 1 can (14 oz / 400g) diced tomatoes, no sugar added
- 2 cups (480ml) chicken broth
- 1 cup (240ml) coconut milk (unsweetened)
- 1 tsp paprika
- 1 tsp cumin
- ½ tsp dried thyme
- ½ tsp black pepper
- ½ tsp salt (or to taste)
- 1 tbsp olive oil
- 1 handful fresh parsley, chopped

Cooking Instructions

Heat olive oil in a pan over medium heat. Brown the ground turkey for 5 minutes, breaking it into small pieces. Transfer to the slow cooker. Add onion, garlic, carrots, celery, sweet potatoes, diced tomatoes, chicken broth, coconut milk, and spices. Stir well. Cover and cook on low for 6 hours or high for 3 hours, until the vegetables are tender. Stir in fresh parsley before serving.

Serving Size

- Makes 4 servings

Nutritional Information (Per Serving)

- Calories: 320
- Protein: 28g
- Carbohydrates: 30g
- Fiber: 6g
- Fat: 10g

Tips

- For a thicker stew, mash some sweet potatoes with a fork before serving.
- If using frozen ground turkey, thaw it first for even cooking.
- Store leftovers in an airtight container for up to 4 days in the fridge.

Possible Variations or Substitutes

- Replace turkey with ground chicken or beef.
- Swap sweet potatoes for butternut squash.
- Use vegetable broth for a lighter taste.

High-Protein Vegan Chili

Ingredients

- 1 cup dried lentils, rinsed
- 1 can (15 oz) black beans, drained and rinsed
- 1 can (15 oz) kidney beans, drained and rinsed
- 1 can (15 oz) diced tomatoes
- 2 cups vegetable broth
- 1 onion, chopped
- 2 cloves garlic, minced
- 1 red bell pepper, chopped
- 1 carrot, chopped
- 1 teaspoon ground cumin
- 1 teaspoon smoked paprika
- 1 teaspoon chili powder
- ½ teaspoon ground coriander
- ½ teaspoon salt (adjust to taste)
- ¼ teaspoon black pepper
- 1 tablespoon olive oil
- 1 tablespoon tomato paste
- ½ teaspoon red pepper flakes (optional, for spice)
- 1 cup corn kernels (fresh or frozen)
- Juice of 1 lime
- ¼ cup fresh cilantro, chopped (optional)

Cooking Instructions

Heat olive oil in a pan over medium heat and sauté onions, garlic, bell pepper, and carrot for 3 minutes. Transfer to the slow cooker. Add lentils, black beans, kidney beans, diced tomatoes, tomato paste, vegetable broth, cumin, paprika, chili powder, coriander, salt, black pepper, and red pepper flakes. Stir well. Cover and cook on low for 6–8 hours or high for 3–4 hours. Stir in corn and lime juice in the last 30 minutes. Adjust seasoning if needed. Garnish with fresh cilantro before serving.

Serving Size

Makes 4–6 servings.

Nutritional Information (Per Serving)

- Calories: 280
- Protein: 15g
- Carbohydrates: 45g
- Fiber: 12g
- Fat: 4g
- Sodium: 420mg

Tips

- Use canned lentils instead of dried to reduce cooking time.
- Add extra spice with jalapeños or cayenne pepper.
- Let the chili sit for a few hours before serving for deeper flavors.

Possible Variations or Substitutes

- Replace lentils with quinoa for a different texture.
- Use pinto beans instead of kidney beans.
- Swap vegetable broth with water and extra seasoning.

SNACKS

➢ Savory Roasted Chickpeas

Ingredients

- 1 can (15 oz / 425g) chickpeas, drained and rinsed
- 1 tablespoon olive oil
- ½ teaspoon salt
- ½ teaspoon black pepper
- ½ teaspoon garlic powder
- ½ teaspoon smoked paprika
- ¼ teaspoon cayenne pepper (optional, for extra spice)

Cooking Instructions

Pat the chickpeas dry with a paper towel. Spread them on a baking tray and let them air-dry for 10 minutes. Put the chickpeas in a bowl and mix with olive oil, salt, pepper, garlic powder, smoked paprika, and cayenne pepper if using. Stir well to coat evenly. Pour the chickpeas into the slow cooker and cook on high for 2–3 hours or until crispy, stirring occasionally. Let them cool before eating.

Serving Size

Makes 4 servings (about ½ cup per serving).

Nutritional Information (Per Serving)

- Calories: 120
- Protein: 5g
- Carbohydrates: 18g
- Fiber: 4g

- Fat: 3.5g
- Sodium: 200mg

Tips

For extra crunch, bake the chickpeas in the oven at 375°F (190°C) for 10 minutes after slow cooking. Store leftovers in an airtight container at room temperature for up to 3 days.

Possible Variations or Substitutes

Use chili powder instead of cayenne for a milder spice. Replace smoked paprika with curry powder for an Indian twist. Swap olive oil for avocado oil for a different flavor. Add a sprinkle of Parmesan cheese after cooking for a cheesy taste.

➤ Slow Cooker Spiced Nuts

Ingredients:

- 2 cups (250g) mixed nuts (almonds, walnuts, pecans, or cashews)
- 2 tablespoons (30g) honey or maple syrup
- 1 tablespoon (15g) melted butter or coconut oil
- 1 teaspoon (2g) ground cinnamon
- ½ teaspoon (1g) ground nutmeg
- ½ teaspoon (1g) ground ginger
- ¼ teaspoon (0.5g) cayenne pepper (optional, for a spicy kick)
- ½ teaspoon (3g) salt
- 1 teaspoon (5ml) vanilla extract

Cooking Instructions:

Place the nuts in the slow cooker. In a small bowl, mix the honey, melted butter, cinnamon, nutmeg, ginger, cayenne pepper, salt, and vanilla extract. Pour the mixture over the nuts and stir until evenly coated. Cover and cook on low for 2 hours, stirring every 30 minutes to prevent burning. Spread the nuts on a baking sheet to cool and harden before storing.

Serving Size:
Makes about 4 servings (½ cup or 60g per serving).

Nutritional Information (Per Serving):

- Calories: 220
- Protein: 5g
- Fat: 18g
- Carbohydrates: 12g
- Fiber: 3g
- Sugar: 7g

Tips:

- Stir regularly to avoid burning, as nuts can cook quickly.
- Let the nuts cool completely before storing to keep them crunchy.
- Store in an airtight container for up to two weeks.

Possible Variations or Substitutes:

- Use almonds only for a milder taste.
- Replace honey with agave syrup for a vegan option.
- Add pumpkin spice for a seasonal flavor.
- Use smoked paprika instead of cinnamon for a savory version.

➤ Homemade Granola Clusters

Ingredients:

- 2 cups (200g) rolled oats
- 1 cup (120g) chopped nuts (almonds, walnuts, or pecans)
- ½ cup (120ml) honey or maple syrup
- ¼ cup (60ml) coconut oil or melted butter
- 1 teaspoon vanilla extract
- ½ teaspoon cinnamon
- ¼ teaspoon salt
- ½ cup (80g) dried fruit (raisins, cranberries, or chopped dates)

Cooking Instructions:

Mix oats, nuts, cinnamon, and salt in a bowl. In another bowl, stir honey, coconut oil, and vanilla until smooth. Pour over the oat mixture and mix well. Line the slow cooker with parchment paper and spread the mixture evenly. Cover and cook on low for 2 to 3 hours, stirring every 30 minutes. Turn off the heat and let the granola cool for 1 hour. Add dried fruit and gently press the mixture to form clusters. Store in an airtight container.

Serving Size:

Makes about 4 cups (8 servings).

Nutritional Information (per serving):

- Calories: 220
- Protein: 4g
- Carbohydrates: 28g
- Fat: 11g
- Fiber: 3g

- Sugar: 12g

Tips:

Let the granola cool completely before storing to keep it crunchy. For extra crispiness, spread the granola on a baking sheet and bake at 300°F (150°C) for 10 minutes after slow cooking.

Variations and Substitutes:

Use sunflower or pumpkin seeds instead of nuts for a nut-free version. Swap honey with agave syrup for a vegan option. Add dark chocolate chips after cooling for a sweet touch.

➤ Low-Sugar Applesauce

Ingredients

- 6 large apples (any variety, peeled, cored, and chopped)
- ½ cup water
- 1 teaspoon cinnamon (optional)
- 1 teaspoon lemon juice
- 1 teaspoon vanilla extract (optional)

Cooking Instructions

Place the chopped apples in the slow cooker. Add water, cinnamon, and lemon juice. Stir to combine. Cover and cook on low for 4–5 hours or until the apples are soft. Mash with a fork for chunky applesauce or blend for a smooth texture. Stir in vanilla extract if using. Let cool before serving or storing.

Serving Size

Makes about 4 cups (8 servings)

Nutritional Information (Per Serving, Approximate)

- Calories: 60
- Carbohydrates: 15g

- Fiber: 3g
- Natural Sugars: 11g
- Protein: 0g
- Fat: 0g

Tips

- Use a mix of apple varieties for a richer flavor.
- If you prefer sweeter applesauce, choose naturally sweet apples like Fuji or Gala.
- Store in the fridge for up to 5 days or freeze for up to 3 months.

Possible Variations or Substitutes

- Add a pinch of nutmeg or ginger for extra flavor.
- Replace water with unsweetened apple juice for a more intense apple taste.
- Use pears instead of apples for a pear sauce variation.

➢ Dark Chocolate Energy Bites

Ingredients:

- 1 cup (100g) rolled oats
- ½ cup (120g) natural peanut butter (or almond butter)
- ⅓ cup (80ml) honey (or maple syrup)
- ¼ cup (25g) unsweetened cocoa powder
- ½ cup (80g) dark chocolate chips (70% or higher)
- 1 teaspoon vanilla extract
- 2 tablespoons (15g) chia seeds (or flaxseeds)
- ¼ teaspoon sea salt

Cooking Instructions:

1. Add all the ingredients to a large mixing bowl.
2. Stir well until everything is combined into a sticky dough.
3. Use your hands or a spoon to scoop small portions and roll them into bite-sized balls.
4. Place the energy bites on a baking sheet lined with parchment paper.
5. Refrigerate for at least 30 minutes to firm up.
6. Store in an airtight container in the fridge for up to one week.

Serving Size:

- Makes about 12 energy bites

Nutritional Information (Per Bite):

- Calories: 120
- Protein: 3g
- Carbohydrates: 15g

- Fat: 6g
- Fiber: 2g
- Sugar: 7g

Tips:

- If the mixture is too dry, add a little more peanut butter or honey.
- If it's too sticky, add more oats or chia seeds.
- Store in the freezer for a longer shelf life.

Possible Variations or Substitutes:

- Swap peanut butter for almond or cashew butter.
- Use agave syrup instead of honey for a vegan option.
- Add chopped nuts, coconut flakes, or dried fruit for extra texture.
- Replace dark chocolate chips with cacao nibs for less sugar.

➢ Protein-Packed Hummus

Ingredients:

- 1 can (15 oz / 400g) chickpeas, drained and rinsed
- ¼ cup (60ml) fresh lemon juice
- ¼ cup (60ml) tahini
- 2 tablespoons olive oil
- 2 garlic cloves, minced
- ½ teaspoon salt
- ½ teaspoon ground cumin
- 2 to 4 tablespoons water (as needed)
- 2 tablespoons Greek yogurt (for extra protein)
- 1 tablespoon hemp seeds or chia seeds (optional, for extra protein)

Cooking Instructions:

Add all the ingredients to the slow cooker. Cook on low for 2 hours or until the chickpeas are very soft. Transfer everything to a blender or food processor. Blend until smooth, adding water as needed for the desired consistency. Serve immediately or refrigerate for later use.

Serving Size:

Makes about 4 servings (¼ cup per serving).

Nutritional Information (Per Serving):

- Calories: 180
- Protein: 8g
- Fat: 10g
- Carbohydrates: 16g

- Fiber: 4g
- Sugar: 1g

Tips:

For a smoother hummus, peel the chickpeas before blending. Add more lemon juice for a tangy flavor. Drizzle extra olive oil on top before serving for a rich taste.

Variations and Substitutes:

- Replace Greek yogurt with silken tofu for a dairy-free version.
- Use black beans instead of chickpeas for a different flavor.
- Add roasted red peppers or sun-dried tomatoes for extra taste.

➢ Chewy Peanut Butter Protein Bars

Ingredients:

- 1 cup (250g) natural peanut butter (unsweetened)
- 1/3 cup (80ml) honey or maple syrup
- 1 teaspoon vanilla extract
- 1 ½ cups (150g) rolled oats
- ½ cup (50g) protein powder (vanilla or unflavored)
- ¼ teaspoon salt
- ¼ cup (40g) dark chocolate chips (optional)
- 2 tablespoons (30ml) milk or almond milk (if needed)

Cooking Instructions:

Melt peanut butter and honey in a small pot over low heat, stirring until smooth. Remove from heat and mix in vanilla extract. In a large bowl, combine oats, protein powder, and salt. Pour the peanut butter mixture over the dry ingredients and stir well. If the mixture is too dry, add a little milk until it holds together. Fold in chocolate chips if using. Press the mixture into a lined 8x8-inch (20x20cm) baking dish. Refrigerate for at least 1 hour until firm. Cut into bars and store in an airtight container.

Serving Size:

Makes 8 bars

Nutritional Information (per bar):

- Calories: 210
- Protein: 10g
- Carbohydrates: 18g
- Fat: 12g
- Fiber: 3g
- Sugar: 7g

Tips:

Use a spoon to press the mixture firmly into the dish to keep the bars from crumbling. Store in the fridge for up to one week or freeze for longer storage. If you prefer a softer texture, let the bars sit at room temperature for a few minutes before eating.

Possible Variations or Substitutes:

Use almond or cashew butter instead of peanut butter. Replace honey with agave syrup for a vegan option. Add nuts, seeds, or dried fruit for extra texture and flavor. Use cocoa powder for a chocolate version.

STEALTH HEALTH TIPS AND TRICKS

Eating healthy doesn't mean sacrificing flavor or spending hours in the kitchen. **Stealth Health** is about making small, smart choices that improve nutrition without making meals feel "diet-friendly" or bland. By using simple tricks, you can add more nutrients, reduce unhealthy ingredients, and enhance flavors without even noticing. Here are some easy and effective tips to help you create healthier meals with minimal effort.

1. Boost Fiber with Whole Grains

Swap white rice, pasta, and bread for whole-grain versions like brown rice, quinoa, whole wheat pasta, or oats. These choices keep you full longer, improve digestion, and provide more vitamins and minerals.

2. Use Natural Sweeteners Instead of Sugar

Refined sugar can cause energy crashes and weight gain. Instead, sweeten your food with honey, maple syrup, mashed bananas, or unsweetened applesauce. These options add natural sweetness along with extra nutrients.

3. Add More Vegetables Without Changing the Taste

Chop or blend veggies into sauces, soups, and stews. Finely grated zucchini, carrots, or spinach can be mixed into pasta sauces, casseroles, and even baked goods without affecting the taste.

4. Cook with Healthy Fats

Replace butter and processed oils with healthier alternatives like olive oil, avocado oil, or coconut oil. These fats are good for your heart and help your body absorb vitamins better.

5. Increase Protein in Your Meals

Adding protein to your meals helps with muscle growth, energy, and satiety. Include lean meats, eggs, beans, tofu, Greek yogurt, or protein powder in your meals. You can also blend protein powder into oatmeal, smoothies, or homemade snacks.

6. Cut Down on Salt Without Losing Flavor

Too much salt can lead to high blood pressure. Instead of using extra salt, season your food with fresh herbs, spices, lemon juice, or vinegar to enhance flavor naturally.

7. Make Meals Creamy Without Heavy Cream

For a creamy texture in soups and sauces, use mashed avocado, blended beans, Greek yogurt, or pureed cauliflower instead of heavy cream. This reduces fat and increases nutrition.

8. Swap Fried for Air-Fried or Baked

Instead of deep-frying, use an air fryer or oven to get crispy textures with less oil. This method keeps food crunchy while cutting down on unhealthy fats.

9. Hydrate Smarter

Skip sugary sodas and juices. Drink more water, herbal teas, or infused water with lemon, mint, or berries for a refreshing and healthy alternative.

10. Plan and Prep for Success

Meal prepping helps you control portions, save time, and make healthier choices. Prepare ingredients in advance, cook in batches, and store meals properly to make healthy eating easier throughout the week.

Healthy eating doesn't have to feel restrictive. By making small, smart swaps, you can enjoy delicious meals while improving your nutrition. These **stealth health** tricks allow you to eat better without even realizing it!

MEAL PREP PLANS

3-Day Meal Plan for Beginners

Day 1

- **Breakfast**: Chewy Peanut Butter Protein Bars
- **Lunch**: Slow Cooker Chicken and Vegetables
- **Dinner**: Slow Cooker Beef Stew
- **Snack**: Roasted Garlic Broccoli
- **Dessert**: Dark Chocolate Energy Bites

Day 2

- **Breakfast**: Overnight Oats with Honey and Nuts
- **Lunch**: Slow Cooker Lentil Soup
- **Dinner**: BBQ Ribs (Combi Crisp)
- **Snack**: Honey-Roasted Carrots
- **Dessert**: Greek Yogurt with Berries

Day 3

- **Breakfast**: Scrambled Eggs with Whole Grain Toast
- **Lunch**: Baked Ziti (Combi Bake)
- **Dinner**: Slow Cooker Herb Chicken
- **Snack**: Peanut Butter Apple Slices
- **Dessert**: Banana Ice Cream

5-Day Meal Plan

Day 1 – See Day 1 from the 3-Day Meal Plan

Day 2 – See Day 2 from the 3-Day Meal Plan

Day 3 – See Day 3 from the 3-Day Meal Plan

Day 4

- **Breakfast**: Avocado Toast with Poached Egg
- **Lunch**: Slow Cooker Shrimp Scampi
- **Dinner**: Air-Fried Pork Tenderloin
- **Snack**: Roasted Root Vegetables
- **Dessert**: Baked Apples with Cinnamon

Day 5

- **Breakfast**: Protein Smoothie with Oats and Banana
- **Lunch**: Slow Cooker Spaghetti Bolognese
- **Dinner**: Chicken and Rice (Rice Function)
- **Snack**: Hummus with Whole-Grain Crackers
- **Dessert**: Dark Chocolate-Covered Almonds

7-Day Meal Plan

Days 1-5 – See the 5-Day Meal Plan

Day 6

- **Breakfast**: Whole Wheat Pancakes with Honey
- **Lunch**: Air-Fried Salmon with Steamed Vegetables
- **Dinner**: Slow Cooker Turkey Chili
- **Snack**: Greek Yogurt with Nuts
- **Dessert**: Peanut Butter Protein Bars

Day 7

- **Breakfast**: Scrambled Eggs with Sautéed Spinach
- **Lunch**: Lasagna (Combi Bake)
- **Dinner**: Air-Fried Beef Roast with Roasted Garlic Broccoli
- **Snack**: Homemade Trail Mix
- **Dessert**: Apple Slices with Almond Butter

14-Day Meal Plan

Days 1-7 – See the 7-Day Meal Plan

Day 8

- **Breakfast**: Smoothie Bowl with Fresh Berries
- **Lunch**: Air-Fried Chicken with Steamed Rice
- **Dinner**: Slow Cooker Vegetable Curry
- **Snack**: Cucumber Slices with Hummus
- **Dessert**: Dark Chocolate Peanut Butter Cups

Day 9

- **Breakfast**: Overnight Chia Pudding
- **Lunch**: Slow Cooker Herb Chicken with Quinoa
- **Dinner**: Shrimp Scampi (Sear/Sauté)
- **Snack**: Air-Fried Sweet Potato Chips
- **Dessert**: Greek Yogurt with Honey

Day 10

- **Breakfast**: Scrambled Tofu with Whole Grain Toast
- **Lunch**: Spaghetti Bolognese (Combi Meals)
- **Dinner**: BBQ Ribs with Roasted Vegetables
- **Snack**: Peanut Butter Banana Bites
- **Dessert**: Baked Apples

Day 11

- **Breakfast**: Oatmeal with Nuts and Dried Fruit
- **Lunch**: Slow Cooker Chickpea Stew

- **Dinner**: Air-Fried Pork Tenderloin
- **Snack**: Roasted Garlic Broccoli
- **Dessert**: Dark Chocolate Bark

Day 12

- **Breakfast**: Whole Grain Waffles with Peanut Butter
- **Lunch**: Slow Cooker Turkey Chili
- **Dinner**: Baked Ziti (Combi Bake)
- **Snack**: Fresh Berries with Almonds
- **Dessert**: Yogurt with Cinnamon

Day 13

- **Breakfast**: Hard-Boiled Eggs with Avocado Toast
- **Lunch**: Slow Cooker Lentil Soup
- **Dinner**: Chicken and Rice (Rice Function)
- **Snack**: Air-Fried Sweet Potato Fries
- **Dessert**: Dark Chocolate-Dipped Strawberries

Day 14

- **Breakfast**: Peanut Butter Protein Bars
- **Lunch**: Air-Fried Beef Roast with Garlic Broccoli
- **Dinner**: Slow Cooker Vegetable Stir-Fry with Tofu
- **Snack**: Hummus with Whole-Grain Crackers
- **Dessert**: Banana Ice Cream

CONCLUSION

Thank you for choosing this book and for taking the time to explore the world of stealth health meal prep. Your commitment to making nutritious and flavorful meals is a step toward a healthier and more enjoyable way of eating. Whether you are new to slow cooker meal prep or have years of experience, every recipe in this book was crafted with simplicity, taste, and health in mind.

As you embark on this journey, remember that cooking is both an art and a skill—one that improves with practice. Follow each recipe carefully, but don't be afraid to make adjustments based on your taste and dietary needs. The tips provided will help you maximize both nutrition and flavor, but you should always feel free to experiment and find what works best for you.

Nobody starts as an expert. Every great cook has had their share of trial and error, and that's perfectly normal. If a recipe doesn't turn out the way you expected the first time, don't be discouraged—try again, tweak the ingredients, and make it your own. The most important thing is that you enjoy the process of cooking and nourishing yourself and your loved ones.

We hope this book has inspired you to make meal prepping easier, healthier, and more enjoyable. Thank you for being a part of this journey, and we wish you success in creating delicious, wholesome meals that fit your lifestyle.

Happy cooking!

Made in the USA
Coppell, TX
13 May 2025